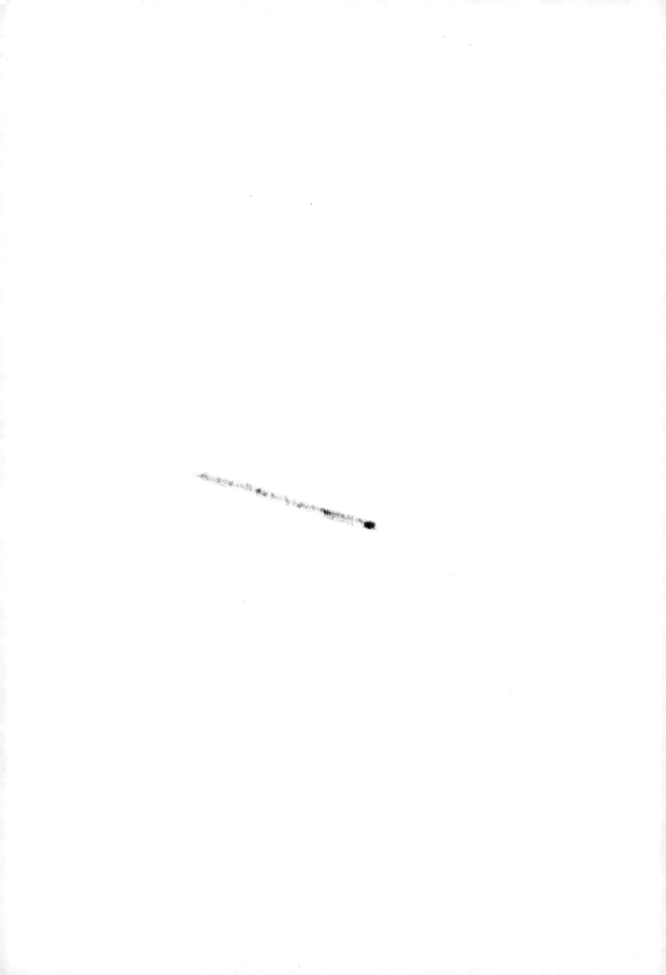

AN
ICE AGE
HUNTER

Series Editor:
Giovanni Caselli

Story Consultant:
Linda Gamlin

Illustrations:
Sergio

Book Editor:
Fiona Macdonald

Series Design:
Caselli Associates

Production:
Susan Mead

First American edition published in 1992 by
Peter Bedrick Books
2112 Broadway
New York, NY 10023

Published by agreement with Simon & Schuster Young Books
Simon & Schuster Ltd, Hemel Hempstead, England

Library of Congress Cataloging-in-Publication Data
Caselli, Giovanni, 1939–
    The everyday life of an ice age hunter / Giovanni Caselli.
    Summary: Reconstructs the seasonal activities and daily life of an
Ice Age tribe in Europe over 15,000 years ago.
    ISBN-0-87226-103-4
    1. Paleolithic period—Europe—Juvenile literature. 2. Europe—
Antiquities—Juvenile literature. [1. Man, Prehistoric.]
I. Title.
GN772.2.A1C37   1992
                                                        91-33261
                                                          CIP
                                                           AC

Printed and bound by
Henri Proost, Turnhout, Belgium
5 4 3 2 1

AN ICE AGE HUNTER

PETER BEDRICK BOOKS

NEW YORK

Contents

Introduction

The people described in this story lived about 15,000 years ago, during the last part of the Ice Age. They lived in Europe; the land where they hunted now forms part of France. They spent the winter months in caves in the centre of the country and trekked westwards to the Atlantic coast every summer.

They travelled around the country in this way because they followed the reindeer herds which lived in northern Europe during the Ice Age. The hunters depended on the reindeer for their survival. Reindeer provided meat, hides for clothes and tents, antlers and bones for tools and fat for lamps. Archaeologists think that each Ice Age adult needed the meat from about 100 reindeer a year to survive. Ice Age hunters invented harpoons and spear throwers to help them catch and kill the animals more easily.

The great herds of reindeer were constantly on the move, looking for fresh grass to eat. The hunters therefore had to follow the reindeer wherever they went. Some tribes of hunters, like the family in this story, made semi-permanent camp sites at places where they thought the reindeer were likely to go during their summer wanderings in search of food.

Remains of these camp sites can still be seen today. We can also see the beautiful paintings of animals with which the hunters decorated their sacred caves. Many flint and bone tools and some fossil remains have survived from the Ice Age period and can be seen in museums. Archaeologists have also studied people who live today in conditions rather like those of Ice Age Europe for clues as to how the Ice Age hunters might have lived.

This book tells the story of a year in the life of an Ice Age child and her family. At the end of the book, you can see some detailed pictures of the tools and equipment that they might have used in their daily life. There are also suggestions for books to read.

Hunting the Reindeer

All winter Jalu had wanted to go with her father to hunt reindeer, but her mother had said she must wait until the new year.

'But how will we know when the new year begins?' Jalu had asked.

'When the snow begins to melt,' her mother had replied, 'and the first patch of earth shows through.'

So every day Jalu looked to see if the snow was melting and, one fine spring day, at last it happened. Jalu was so excited that she danced round the cave.

'You can't come with us if you're going to act like that,' said her father sharply. 'You must keep very quiet when we get near the herd or you'll scare them away. Then we'll never catch them.'

The day of the hunt dawned bright and clear. Her mother wrapped Jalu in a fur coat and told her to do exactly what her father said.

They set off, and soon reached the place where the reindeer were grazing, shovelling aside the snow with their great wide hooves to get at the moss underneath. Jalu was told to hide behind a tree. Her father and uncles spread out in a line and moved slowly forward.

At first the reindeer took no notice. Then they stopped eating and began to look around. They knew that something was wrong but for a moment they did not move. All the while the hunters edged closer.

Suddenly, the reindeer began to run. At the same time, a spear flew through the air, then another and another. One spear struck the animal nearest to the hunters and it bellowed loudly. Then another spear hit its side and the reindeer fell. As the herd stampeded away, the hunters ran towards the wounded animal. It tried to struggle to its feet and escape, but it was too weak. The hunters closed in around it.

After that Jalu could not see what was happening but she heard the reindeer bellowing and the men shouting. Then everything went quiet and she knew the animal was dead. Her father signalled her to come over and asked her to clean his stone knife for him. Then they loaded the dead animal on to the sledge and Jalu helped to haul it back to the cave.

Following the Herd

One morning Jalu woke up very early, before it was really light. She felt much too excited to go back to sleep because she knew that today they would be leaving for the sea. They would follow the reindeer herd, which had started its long journey south.

Jalu lay awake and thought about the stories her grandfather had told them the night before. They had been sitting round the fire in the cave, looking out at the bright starry sky.

'The stars are the spirits of our ancestors,' Grandfather said. 'When our ancestors died they went up into the sky to be with the moon, our first ancestor. They roam about the sky looking for the reindeer herds, just as we follow the reindeer down here.

8

'Like us, they hunt for the reindeer to give them meat and hides for their tents and all the other things they need. But there are no reindeer up there, so they go wandering round and round for ever. That is why the stars move round the sky.'

'Then they must get very hungry,' Jalu said.

'No,' replied Grandfather, 'they feel no hunger up there and they are never cold. Not like us.'

During the winter it had been very cold in the cave, even with a fire blazing all the time. Jalu and her family had sometimes felt hungry, too, when the hunters hadn't managed to catch enough for everyone to eat. But now the winter was over. The reindeer were on the move. Jalu's cousin, Natho, had been watching the herd, and last night he brought good news. The reindeer were on their way to the coast where they always spent the summer! Today Jalu's family would be leaving too, following the herd to the sea.

As soon as it was light, everyone got up and began work. Jalu was sent to fill the waterskins at the stream while her parents packed all their belongings into big bundles. Then the sledges were loaded up with the heavy reindeer hides which they needed to make the tents.

'Shall I carry something?' Jalu asked, as they set off.

'No,' said her mother, 'there's a long journey ahead. You'll need all your strength for walking.'

The Summer Camp

The journey to the sea was very long and hard. Jalu's legs had ached with all the walking and sometimes her feet were so sore she felt she couldn't go any farther. Everyone was tired and bad-tempered.

But early one morning they had come over a hill and suddenly they had seen the wonderful blue sea, stretching away in the distance. Everyone shouted for joy at the sight. Soon they arrived at the place on the beach where they always camped, and everyone was happy again.

'Do you see this stone floor?' Jalu's mother said, as she put down her bundle. 'It was made by our ancestors. As long as we come back here we will always have somewhere safe and dry to sleep.'

Father went off to chop down some young trees for tent poles. He pushed them firmly into the holes between the stone slabs. Then he wove thin branches between the poles and arranged the skins carefully over them. Jalu and her cousins collected pebbles from the beach to hold the skins down.

Mother told the children to go and collect firewood before it got too dark. They found lots of dead branches underneath the old pine trees upon the cliff.

Jalu always liked to watch a fire being made. First her mother got out the special stones that she used to make fire. She piled up dry leaves and struck the stones together over them, saying the magic words that mean 'Fire come! Fire come!' A spark leaped out, the leaves crackled and smoke began to pour from them. Mother blew gently on the leaves. A flame appeared, grew bigger and was soon burning brightly.

'Now can we go and paddle?' Jalu asked when the fire was lit. But her mother said it was too late, and the water would be icy cold.

'Wait until tomorrow.'

Salmon Fishing

The weather was getting warmer and warmer. The children could paddle and swim every day and the cliffs were covered with flowers. Jalu's eldest sister, Sonda, took her to look for a special flower, a tiny pink one shaped like a star. When they found it she was very pleased.

'If this flower is open,' Sonda said, 'it means that it's time for the salmon to be leaping up the river.'

The next day, Sonda, Jalu and their cousins got up very early and set off for the river where there was a salmon leap. The younger children had to stay at home, because lions and bears sometimes hunted by the river.

They walked along the beach to where the river flowed into the sea. They turned inland and walked along the riverbank for many hours, until they came to a place where the water tumbled down over some rocks in a series of little waterfalls.

'This is where we'll catch the salmon,' said Sonda. Just as she spoke a huge silvery fish leaped out of the water and plunged back in with a great splash. Then another jumped, and another. When the fourth one jumped, Natho, Jalu's cousin, hurled his harpoon, piercing the fish in mid-air. The salmon struggled and twisted about as it fell back into the stream, taking the harpoon with it. Jalu was afraid that the harpoon would be swept away with the salmon, but Natho had the harpoon rope held firmly in his hand. He pulled hard on the rope and dragged the fish up on to the bank.

By nightfall they had 12 salmon piled up in a basket. Sonda had just learned from their mother how to make fire, so she lit a fire and cooked two salmon for their supper. They were delicious.

'Do we have to go back tomorrow?' Jalu asked.

'No,' said Sonda, 'we must stay here another day and catch more fish.'

During the night there were many strange noises – howling, roaring and snarling. Sonda told Jalu not to be frightened. But she added more wood to the fire.

'The animals are afraid of the flames,' she said. 'They won't come near us if we keep the fire burning.'

New Clothes

Jalu and Tamar sat on the beach and watched the sun go down over the sea.

'Where does the sun go at night?' Tamar asked. Jalu's grandmother was very old and wise. She told them.

'At night,' Grandmother explained, 'the sun falls into the sea and is swallowed by a giant fish. The fish swims underneath the world and then he coughs up the sun on the other side.'

Grandmother continued her story. 'The world is floating on the sea. This is the edge of the world here. And the place we go to in winter, where the caves are, is the centre of the world. Everywhere else there's just sea and sky.'

While she talked, Grandmother was sewing pieces of hide together with a bone needle.

'What are you doing, Grandmother?' asked Jalu.

'I'm making you a new tunic,' she replied, 'All you children have grown so much. You all need new clothes. It's going to be a lot of work making them.'

Jalu's mother and aunts were busy preparing the reindeer hides for Grandmother to sew. First they scraped the insides of the skins clean. Then they beat them to make them softer, and stretched them out to dry in the sun. When they were ready, Grandmother sewed them together. She made Jalu try the new tunic on for size.

'Could you sew some shells on it?' Jalu asked.

'Of course I will, if you find some. But I can't look for them, I'm much too busy.'

So Jalu ran off to look for shells. Then she caught sight of her father and went to see what he was doing. He had already made a pile of bone needles and fish hooks. Now he had a big shell in one hand and he was turning a drill with the other to make a hole in the shell. He had made some beads as well, from teeth and pieces of bone.

'You can have some of these beads to sew on your tunic if you like,' he said, 'and I'll make you some more for a necklace.'

A Summer Feast

'Tonight there will be a full moon, so we ought to have a feast,' said Grandmother. Everyone agreed.

'We must have some other meat as well as reindeer,' Jalu's father pointed out, 'because it's a special occasion.' So he took his bow and arrows and set off to hunt for birds.

Jalu's elder brother, Samo, went to look for mussels and limpets and other shellfish on the beach. Sonda went up to the clifftop searching for herbs and fresh young leaves to eat with the meat. Jalu's mother went off to the woods to pick berries. She knew which ones were good and which ones you shouldn't touch. Meanwhile Jalu and her cousins collected lots of firewood.

After the sun went down, the fires were started and soon the beach was brightly lit by the flames. The birds and the joints of reindeer meat were put on spits over the fire to cook. Jalu's mother pounded the berries she had picked between two stones, to make them into sauce.

16

'This will make the meat taste really good,' she said.

She was right. Jalu thought that all the food tasted wonderful. When everyone had eaten as much as they possibly could, they sang songs and danced around the fires. Then the moon came up, huge and yellow at first. Slowly it rose into the sky and its silvery light glinted on the sea.

Later on, in bed in the tent, Jalu lay awake for a long time listening to the others singing and telling stories. When at last the feast was over and her parents came into the tent, she pretended to be asleep. Jalu heard them talking in low voices. What they said made her feel sad. She didn't want to leave the summer camp.

'That was the fourth full moon since we've been here,' said her mother, 'so summer will be over soon and the reindeer will be moving on. We must set off before them. There are so many things to be done at the autumn camp. If we don't go soon we'll never be ready for winter.'

'Yes, I suppose you're right,' sighed her father. 'We'll make a start tomorrow.'

The Autumn Camp

It wasn't far to the autumn camp – only two days walking. They found a beautiful spot to put up their tents, among some birch trees beside a stream.

'I like this place,' said Jalu dreamily. 'It will be lovely staying here.'

'There won't be much time to enjoy yourself,' said her mother. 'We have to work hard from now on. The winter is coming and if we're not ready for it we will all die of cold or hunger. Tomorrow I'm going out to pick nuts and berries. You can come and help me with that.'

Jalu's father went fishing. By the time Jalu and her mother got back to the camp, he was busy splitting the fish open and hanging them above the fire.

'What are you doing that for?' asked Jalu.

'So that the fish will keep all through the winter,' said her father. 'The smoke from the fire gets inside them and they stay good to eat.'

The next day Jalu helped her cousins to make rope. They collected the longest grass stems they could find and twisted them tightly together. The sharp edges of the grass blades hurt Jalu's fingers, but her mother said she must keep on until the rope was finished.

'There's not much more to do now, Jalu,' said her mother, later on. 'Would you like to go with your uncles? They're going to the woods to check their traps.'

So Jalu set off with her uncles. They hoped to catch lots of rabbits and foxes because the family needed plenty of warm furs for the winter.

One trap was in a clearing in the wood, and as they got near to it they saw a group of bison grazing there. The huge male was snorting and bellowing and rubbing his head against a tree as if he were very angry.

'Shall we run away?' Jalu whispered. 'The bison might attack us.'

'No, don't worry,' her uncle replied. 'He won't hurt us. He knows we are people of the Bison Tribe. He'll bring good luck to our traps.'

When they got back, Jalu's mother was collecting up the smoked fish and packing them into a basket.

'Come on, you must help to pack up,' she said. 'Natho says that he has seen the reindeer herd on the horizon. As soon as they get here we must be ready to follow them.'

The Homecoming

The first snow had fallen. When Jalu woke up it was bitterly cold inside the tent. It was many days since they had left the autumn camp, so many that Jalu had lost count. And now the winter had arrived sooner than expected.

'Do you think there's much farther to go?' wondered Samo.

'No,' said their mother coming into the tent with extra furs. 'I recognize this place. We're quite near our winter caves. We should reach them today if we set out early.'

So they walked without stopping all morning and by the afternoon they could just see their caves in the distance. As they got nearer to them Jalu heard voices and saw fires burning.

When at last they arrived they were greeted with loud shouts, and some people that they knew came running to meet them. Jalu and her family were helped up the slope to the cave, and invited to sit around the fire and get warm. There was roast meat, too, and fresh water to drink.

Like Jalu and her family, these people were members of the Bison Tribe. They came back here every winter but in the summer they always went south, following a different reindeer herd.

The two families talked for a long time about all the things that had happened during the summer. At last Jalu's father stood up.

'We must start work on our cave now,' he said, 'or we won't be safe by nightfall.'

Although nobody wanted to, they left the warm fireside and set to work. Jalu's father and uncles cut down some trees to block off the cave entrance. When they had dragged the trees up to the cave, they propped them against the cave mouth and held them in place with large stones. Then they spread the reindeer hides over them and lashed them down with ropes to keep out the wind and snow.

'I think this is the rope you made in the autumn,' Jalu's father shouted to her. 'I hope you made it well, or we'll know who to blame when the hides come loose and we all freeze to death!'

The Bison Hunt

For Jalu and her family, winter was the hardest part of the year. But it was also a very exciting time, because this was when all their ceremonies took place and there was lots of feasting and dancing.

'Tomorrow at full moon, the most important ceremony of the year will take place,' Grandmother told Jalu. 'We will ask the spirit of the bison to come and live in our sacred cave for another year. Today is the first part of the ceremony when the men go to hunt the bison.'

'But they wouldn't kill a bison, would they?' Jalu asked her. 'Isn't the bison our special friend?'

'They won't kill its spirit,' Grandmother replied, 'only its body. They have to hunt it in a very special way to do this. See, they're getting ready now.'

She took Jalu inside their cave, where her father and uncles and elder brother Samo were all sitting by the fire. They were singing strange songs in low voices. Grandfather stood over them, decorating their faces with red earth. He was chanting too. They looked very frightening and Jalu ran outside again.

She had to wait until the next evening to hear about the hunt from Samo.

'We went down to the woods,' he said, 'all the men of our tribe together, singing the songs of the bison. The magician led us to where the bison were feeding.

The magician is a great leader of our tribe. He can talk to the bison in their own language. He asked them to come back with us, back to our sacred cave. He told them that we would pierce them with our spears, and kill their bodies, but that their spirits would not die.'

'And are they going to come to the cave?' Jalu asked.

'Yes,' said Samo. 'There are two of them ready to come. Tomorrow we'll go and fetch them.'

The Magician's Dance

The next morning all the people of the Bison Tribe gathered in the valley. Jalu saw the magician standing talking to the hunters who had killed the bison. He drew his long dark cloak around him and led everyone towards the wood. There they found the two bison that Samo had described. The men tied strong ropes around the bodies. Then they dragged them back to the caves over the icy ground.

After sunset, the fires were lit and everyone gathered round to hear the magician recite his spells over the two bison. Then he took out a sharp stone knife and held it above the bigger animal. They watched as he cut off the huge bison's head and stripped the hide from its body.

Slowly, very slowly, the magician stood up and lifted the bison head high above his own so that everyone could see it. Then he stooped forward, balancing the great head on his shoulders, and began to dance. All the time he was singing in a strange voice. As he moved between the fires, the flickering light cast strange, gigantic shadows of the bison-man against the rocks. Faster and faster he went, dancing and jumping, round and round, singing all the time.

Then suddenly he ran away from the fires, into the dark night.

'He's going to the sacred cave now,' said Jalu's mother, 'come on, we must go with him.' Jalu followed the others as they hurried through a narrow opening in the rock then down long, twisting passageways, on and on, deep underground.

24

It was dark and damp and she grazed her hand on the rock as she passed.

At last the narrow tunnel opened out into a wide cavern. Here the magician began his dance again and the men followed him, some carrying lamps of burning fat, others waving their spears. As they danced, they sang, but Jalu could not understand the words. Her hand was hurting and she was very frightened to be so far underground.

'What does the song mean?' Jalu asked her mother.

'They are asking the spirit of the bison to live here and be happy,' her mother replied.

Cave Painting

At first it was so dark in the cave that Jalu could hardly see anything, just the men circling round with their flickering lamps. But after a while her eyes got used to the darkness, and then she looked around her. For a moment she could not believe what she saw. All over the walls there were animals, huge animals: bison and horses, bulls and stags, all leaping and prancing about. Her mother saw Jalu staring at them.

'They are pictures painted by the tribes in our valley – the people of the Horse Tribe and the Bull Tribe and many others,' she whispered. 'They all bring the spirits of their sacred animals to live here. Do you see that bison on the wall there?' Jalu looked and saw an enormous snorting bison painted in red and black.

'That's the one we brought to the cave last winter,' her mother said. 'This year there are two bison so we will have to paint pictures of them both.'

Just then Tamar began to cry, saying that he was cold. Jalu shivered, as well. It was chilly in the cave.

'You must both be hungry, too,' said their mother, putting her arms around him and Jalu. 'Let's go and have something to eat and warm up by the fire. We can come back later and watch the men painting.'

But it was a long walk to the fire and back, and Tamar's short legs could not carry him very quickly. So by the time they got back to the sacred cave, the paintings were nearly finished. In the corner sat the magician, still chanting, but very softly now. The heavy bison's head was gone and he was wearing a smaller head-dress of horns. His eyes were closed and he seemed to be in a trance. Two of Jalu's uncles were pounding red and black earth into powder and mixing up the last lot of paint for the artists. The magician looked exhausted and so did all the other men. It had been a very long ceremony and now it was almost over.

'Tonight they will want to sleep, but tomorrow we will celebrate with a feast,' said Jalu's mother. 'The spirit of the bison is back in the cave, and we will all have good luck for another year.'

Picture Glossary

Food and animals

Ice Age hunters depended on reindeer for their survival. Reindeer provided meat, hides for clothes and tents, antlers and bones for tools and fat for lamps.

Although reindeer meat made up over three-quarters of the hunters' diet, they also hunted other herd animals (pictured below) for meat. Wolves, bears and foxes were trapped for their fur.

Flint Tools

Ice Age hunters and craftworkers were successful because they made better and more efficient tools than earlier hunters and trappers. Many of their tools were made from bone, but heavy-duty cutting and boring tools were made from flint. Flints with a naturally sharp edge were used as scrapers. Pointed flints, or burins, were used to drill eyes in bone needles. Other flints could be made into sawing tools. The toolmaker held the flint firmly on a working surface and struck it with a stone to break off a flake. The edges of the flake were chipped with an antler tool.

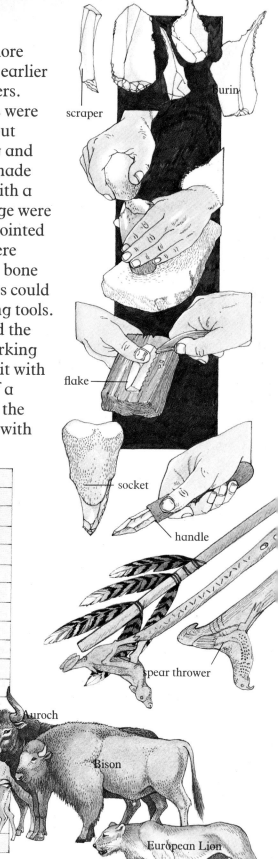

scraper

burin

flake

socket

handle

spear thrower

Reindeer

Auroch

Red deer

Horse

Bison

Brown bear

Roe deer

Wolf

Fox

European Lion

Assembling the spear

Spearheads or barbed harpoons were fitted onto a long wooden spear shaft, the base of which slotted into the grooves in the spear-thrower. This was a kind of 'launcher' to help the hunter throw the spear further.

To keep the wooden spear shaft true it was pushed through the hole in the spear straightener.

spear straightener

Throwing the spear

A leather thong attached the spear-thrower to the hunter's wrist. As he hurled the spear he flicked his wrist, giving extra thrust.

harpoon

spear head

Bone needles

Many needles have been found from this time. They were used to sew animal hides to make clothes and shoes. The needles were made from splinters of reindeer or other bone. The eyes of the needle were made with the point of a flint burin rotated in the wide end of the splinter. The sides of the needle were smoothed with a serrated flint tool. To finish, the needle was turned in grooves cut in a sandstone block.

Drilling tool

The wooden and bone drill below was used to make holes in bone and shells for jewellery. Eskimos still use this kind of drill.

29

Finding Out More

Books to Read

The following books contain information about the
Ice Age period:

G. Caselli **The First Civilizations** (History of
Everyday Things series) Peter Bedrick Books 1985
B. Cox **Prehistoric Animals** (Knowledge Through
Color series) Bantam 1971
N. Merriman **Early Humans** (Eyewitness Books)
Knopf 1989

These four books describe the lives of Eskimo and
American Indian peoples in the recent past. They can
help us to understand what it might have been like to
live in conditions similar to those found in the Ice Age:
N. Bancroft-Hunt **The Indians of the Great Plains**
Peter Bedrick Books 1989
N. Bancroft-Hunt **People of the Totem** Peter Bedrick
Books 1989
M. Wood **North American Indian Mythology**
(Library of the World's Myths and Legends) Peter
Bedrick Books 1985
M. Wood **Spirits, Heroes & Hunters from North
American Indian Mythology** (The World Mythology
Series) Peter Bedrick Books 1992

PRINTED IN BELGIUM BY

proost
INTERNATIONAL BOOK PRODUCTION